Exercise and Play

Ryan Wheatcroft   Katie Woolley

WAYLAND

First published in Great Britain in 2017 by Wayland

Copyright © Hodder and Stoughton, 2017

Editor: Victoria Brooker
Designer: Anthony Hannant, Little Red Ant

ISBN: 978 1 5263 0492 6 (hbk)
ISBN: 978 1 5263 0493 3 (pbk)

10 9 8 7 6 5 4 3 2 1

Wayland, an imprint of
Hachette Children's Group
Part of Hodder and Stoughton
Carmelite House
50 Victoria Embankment
London EC4Y 0DZ

An Hachette UK Company
www.hachette.co.uk
www.hachettechildrens.co.uk

Printed and bound in China

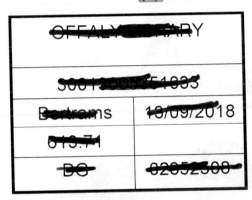

MIX
Paper from
responsible sources
FSC® C104740
FSC
www.fsc.org

Contents

Exercise and Play

Exercise and play help to keep you fit and healthy. Being active uses your body and makes it work better. Exercise helps to build a strong body that will do all the things you want it to do.

You can have lots of fun keeping fit. You can play with your friends and take part in sports. The more active you are, the healthier you will be.

Ready, Steady, Go!

It can be easy not to be active — there are cars, trains and buses to get from place to place, and plenty of video games to play and television programmes to watch. But the human body is meant to be active — without exercise, it starts to slow down and become unhealthy.

You probably get some exercise everyday without even knowing about it. When you run about with your friends or skip in the playground, you are exercising!

Get Up, Get Active

Did you know that the more active you are, the more energy you will have? The more exercise you do, the less tired you will be! And your body will become stronger and fitter.

Exercise can also make you happy! When you exercise, your brain releases chemicals called endorphins, which make you feel happier.

Healthy Heart

Your heart is a muscle that pumps blood and oxygen to all the cells in your body. Every day of your life, your heart is working very hard. It needs to be fit and strong to do its job!

When you exercise, your body needs more oxygen than usual, so your heart has to work even harder — it is getting its own workout! This helps keep your heart healthy.

Lovely Lungs

Your lungs have an important job to do, too. They take in the oxygen your body needs to work properly. This oxygen then goes to your heart, which pumps it around your body in your blood.

When you exercise, your breathing quickens as your lungs take in more oxygen. This oxygen reaches your muscles and helps them work hard so that your body can be as active as possible.

Strength and Stretch

Being active strengthens all the muscles in your body. Do you like jumping on a trampoline or riding a bike? These activities build up your body's strength.

Exercise and play also help your body bend and stretch easily.

Activities such as gymnastics, ballet and martial arts are very good at keeping your body flexible.

Brilliant Brain

Keeping your body busy and active gets the blood flowing, so more oxygen can get to your brain. This can help your brain to think better and you will be able to concentrate more at school.

Being active also helps you sleep. When you exercise, your brain gets the message that you're tired at night. You'll wake up feeling refreshed!

Games to Play

It's lots of fun exercising with friends. Why not take part in team sports such as football or rugby to keep fit? You'll learn a new skill and have fun at the same time!

You can also keep fit and healthy when you are at the park. Riding your scooter, swinging on the monkey bars and kicking a ball are all great ways to play and exercise.

Running and Swimming

Running strengthens your leg muscles and gets blood pumping around your body. Running very fast is called sprinting. Running a long way at a slower pace is called long-distance running.

Swimming is great fun, too! Lots of muscles in your body get a good workout when you are in the water. Learning to swim means you can have all sorts of water fun, from swimming and diving to kayaking and surfing.

Throwing and Climbing

Playing throwing and catching games with your friends is a good way to keep your body active. These games also help develop your hand-eye coordination skills. Being able to guide your hands with your eyes helps you do all sorts of things more easily, such as writing and tying your shoelaces!

Climbing frames and climbing walls are great places to practise your balance skills. Balancing is being able to hold your body in a certain position for a certain length of time. Yoga is another form of exercise that develops balance.

Food and Water

Your body needs energy to exercise and play. You get energy from the food you eat. Drinking water also helps your busy body to breathe, walk, play and grow.

Healthy food keeps your bones nice and strong so they can help you move. Being active and eating healthily makes all the different parts of your body stay fit and healthy, from your heart and lungs to your leg and arm muscles.

Exercising Safely

It's important to wear the right clothes when you are active, such as your helmet when riding your bike. If it's hot, wear shorts and a t-shirt. When it's colder outside, wear layers that you can take off when you start to feel warm.

Have a drink of water before you start exercising and stretch to warm up your muscles. Then, have a snack and another drink when you have finished. Most of all, have fun!

Top Tips!

Try to be active for an hour a day. You don't have to do it all at once. You could ride your bike to school, play hopscotch at lunchtime and go for a walk after dinner!

Don't be a couch potato! Get up and move about for fifteen minutes every two hours.

When you wake each morning, take a big stretch to flex those muscles!

Play outside as much as you can — there is more room to run around and make a noise. Fresh air is good for your lungs and your whole body.

Parents' and Teachers' Notes

This book is designed for children to begin to learn about the importance of being healthy, and the ways in which we can look after our bodies to keep fit and well. Read the book with children either individually or in groups. Don't forget to talk about the pictures as you go.

Whether it's walking to school or scoring a rugby try, there are lots of ways to have fun and exercise at the same time. Here are some discussion topics to encourage further thinking about exercise and play:

 How does your body move every day? What does it feel like to stretch in the morning? How does running make your body feel?

 How do you feel after you've done some exercise? Do you feel good or bad?

 Can you tell me about different kinds of exercise? What counts as exercise? Does nodding your head count? Why or why not?

 What is your favourite sport to play?

If you don't enjoy sport or find it hard, what other ways can you think of to exercise?

Activities you can do

 Try keeping a log of the exercise you do each day. You'll be surprised how busy you are!

 Why not set up an obstacle course with your friends. You could include a hula hoop station, an egg and spoon race and a scooter race!

Further reading

Fact Cat: Healthy Eating by Izzi Howell (Wayland, 2017)
First Sport: Martial Arts by James Nixon *(Watts, 2016)*
Mad About: Dance by Judith Heneghan (Wayland, 2016)
Mad About: Football by Judith Heneghan
 (Wayland, 2016)
Mad About: Swimming by Judith Heneghan
 (Wayland, 2016)
Mad About: Gymnastics by Judith Heneghan
 (Wayland, 2016)

Glossary

blood the red fluid that moves through the heart and around your body, carrying important minerals and oxygen to and waste material from the parts of the body

cell the basic unit of the body that makes up all living things

endorphin a chemical that is released in the brain. Endorphins trigger a positive feeling in your body

flexible to bend your body easily

hand-eye coordination the ability to use your eyes to direct your hands to do a specific task. You use hand-eye coordination to eat your food with a fork and to catch a ball

lungs an organ in your body that takes in oxygen and removes carbon dioxide

muscle a tissue in the body that helps you move a specific part of your body

oxygen a gas found in the air that is necessary to live

Index

Healthy Me Titles in the series

Eating Well
Ryan Wheatcroft · Katie Woolley

You Are What You Eat?
Where Does Your Food Go?
What Are Vitamins And Minerals?
Carbohydrates and Protein
Milk & Dairy, Fats & Sugars
Fruit and Vegetables
Water
Ready, Set, Breakfast
Lunchtime
Dinner is Served!
Snack Attack!
Ditch the Junk
Top Tips!
Parents' and Teachers' Notes
Glossary and Index

Exercise and Play
Ryan Wheatcroft · Katie Woolley

Exercise and Play
Ready, Steady, Go!
Get Up, Get Active
Healthy Heart
Lovely Lungs
Strength and Stretch
Brilliant Brain
Games to Play
Running and Swimming
Throwing and Climbing
Food and Water
Exercising Safely
Top Tips!
Parents' and Teachers' Notes
Glossary and Index

Keeping Clean
Ryan Wheatcroft · Katie Woolley

Your Amazing Body
Germs Everywhere
Feeling Sick
Clean Hands
Clean Hair
Clean Teeth
Clean Feet
Noses and Nails
Easy Ears
Keeping Clean After Sports
Clean Clothes
Why Do I Need to Clean My Room?
Top Tips!
Parents' and Teachers' Notes
Glossary and Index

Keeping Safe
Ryan Wheatcroft · Katie Woolley

Wonderful World
At Home
Out And About
On The Road
Near Water
Whatever The Weather
What's In Your Mouth?
Safety Online
Stranger Danger
My Body, My Rules
Friends Or Foes!
Emergency, Emergency
Top Tips!
Parents' and Teachers' Notes
Glossary and Index

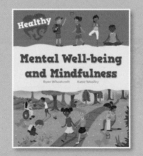

Mental Well-being and Mindfulness
Ryan Wheatcroft · Katie Woolley

What Is Mental Wellbeing?
Your Mind Matters
What Are Mental Health Problems?
Stress And Anxiety
Dealing With Change
It's Good To Talk
Love And Affection
Give Your Self-Esteem A Boost
Nurturing Your Mental Wellbeing
What Is Mindfulness?
Mindfulness Matters
Mindfulness Activities
Top Tips!
Parents' and Teachers' Notes
Glossary and Index

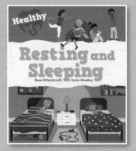

Resting and Sleeping
Ryan Wheatcroft · Katie Woolley

Why Do We Need To Sleep And Rest?
How Much Sleep Do I Need?
A Lack Of Sleep
Day And Night
Sleep Stages
Drift Off To Dreamland
Take Time To Wind Down
Screen Time
A Restful Room
I Just Don't Feel Tired
Rest And Relax
Yoga Calm
Top Tips!
Parents' and Teachers' Notes
Glossary and Index